Fine Art Photographs

Decades of being around accomplished talent producing absolutely phenomenal quality work has taught that we are capable of greatness. It is possible to meet our destiny and become it. Experiencing excellence done with such apparent ease and humble selfless gratification is the motivation for this original photography. Most important was having the freedom.

Being colorblind gives an advantage when composing black & white… less confusion. This special collection selected from thousands of captures. All images were framed in the camera and presented without edits, genuine as seen through the lens. RAW conversion applied by proprietary panchromatic process from source files.

Limited edition prints and custom work available.

info@ BEACHNOISE.com

Joseph Fleming

0125

0351

0437

0780

0826

1085

1581

1608

1976

2068

2089

2180

2397

2467

2495

2962

3147

3151

3359

3656

3714

3881

3916

3937

3943

4035

4070

4193

4533

5492

5705

5708

5750

5811

5844

5846

7182

7656

7693

7783

7843

8345

8407

8470

8471

8889

9024

9353

9430

9970

9975

9980

9995

9998

10002

www.ingramcontent.com/pod-product-compliance
Lightning Source LLC
Chambersburg PA
CBHW040847180526
45159CB00001B/344